To ....

From ....

Compiled by Andrea Skevington
Illustrations copyright © 2004 The Wright Sisters
This edition copyright © 2004 Lion Hudson

A Lion Book
an imprint of
Lion Hudson plc
Mayfield House, 256 Banbury Road,
Oxford OX2 7DH, England
www.lionhudson.com
ISBN 0 7459 5162 7

First edition 2004
1 3 5 7 9 10 8 6 4 2 0

Acknowledgments

Page 52: Proverbs 16:24, from the *Holy Bible, New International Version*, copyright ©
1973, 1978, 1984 International Bible Society. Used by permission of Zondervan and
Hodder & Stoughton Limited. All rights reserved. The 'NIV' and 'New International Version'
trademarks are registered in the United States Patent and Trademark Office by International
Bible Society. Use of either trademark requires the permission of International Bible Society.
UK trademark number 1448790. Every effort has been made to trace and acknowledge
copyright holders of all the quotations in this book. We apologize for any errors or omissions
that may remain, and would ask those concerned to contact the publishers, who will ensure
that full acknowledgment is made in the future.

A catalogue record for this book is available
from the British Library

Typeset in 16/22 Aunt Mildred
Printed and bound in Singapore

happiness

Compiled by
Andrea Skevington
Illustrated by
The Wright Sisters

A LION BOOK

Happiness...

it's what everyone's looking for!

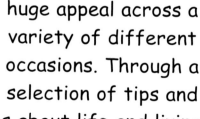

This is a gift book with huge appeal across a variety of different occasions. Through a selection of tips and quotations about life and living it looks at what happiness is, why it's so important and how we can find it. Helpful thoughts on living life combined with heartwarming illustrations make this a book that's hard to resist.

1

Happiness is...
having something
to hope for

The only joy in the world is to begin.

Cesare Pavese

The future belongs to those who believe
in the beauty of the dream.

Eleanor Roosevelt

Hope is a gift we give ourselves,
and it remains when all else is gone.

Naomi Judd

Dream as if you'll live for ever.

Live as if you'll die today.

James Dean

2

Happiness is...
having something
to accomplish

If you do a good job for others,

you heal yourself at the same time,

because a dose of joy is a spiritual cure.

Dietrich Bonhoeffer

Where there is hate, let me sow love;

where there is injury, pardon;

where there is doubt, faith;

where there is despair, hope;

where there is darkness, light.

St Francis of Assisi

It is not doing the things we like to do,

but liking the things we have to do

that makes life blessed.

Anon

3

Happiness is...

having someone to love

Life is to be fortified by many friendships.

To love and to be loved

is the greatest happiness

of existence.

Sydney Smith

There is no surprise more magical than
the surprise of being loved; it is God's finger
on man's shoulder.

Charles Morgan

Treasure the love you receive above all.
It will survive long after your gold and
good health have vanished.

Og Mandino

4

Happiness is...
listening to music

Take a music bath once or twice a week for
a few seasons, and you will find that it is to
the soul what the water bath is to the body.

Oliver Wendell Holmes

A man should hear a little music, read a
little poetry, and see a fine picture every day
of his life, in order that worldly cares may not
obliterate the sense of the beautiful which God
has implanted in the human soul.

Johann Wolfgang von Goethe

I think I should have no other mortal wants,
if I could always have plenty of music. It seems
to infuse strength into my limbs and ideas into
my brain. Life seems to go on without effort,
when I am filled with music.

George Eliot

5

Happiness is...
learning something new

Somewhere, something incredible is
waiting to be known.

Blaise Pascal

Try to learn something about everything
and everything about something.

Thomas H. Huxley

Use what talents you possess. The woods
would be very silent if no birds sang there
except those that sang best.

William Blake

Life is like playing a violin in public and
learning the instrument as one goes on.

Samuel Butler

6

Happiness is...
laughing

Don't wait to be happy to laugh...
You may die and never have laughed!

Jean de La Bruyère

Those who can laugh without cause have
either found the true meaning of happiness
or have gone stark raving mad.

Norm Papernick

The person who can bring the spirit of
laughter into a room is indeed blessed.

Bennett Alfred Cerf

Even if happiness forgets you a little bit,
never completely forget about it.

Jacques Prévert

7

Happiness is...
being somewhere
beautiful

My soul can find no staircase to heaven

unless it be through earth's loveliness.

Michelangelo

Beauty awakens the soul to act.

Dante Alighieri

A rock pile ceases to be a rock pile

the moment a single man contemplates it,

bearing within him the image of a cathedral.

Antoine de Saint-Exupéry

What a man takes in by contemplation,

that he pours out in love.

Meister Eckhart

A thing of beauty is a joy for ever:

Its loveliness increases; it will never

Pass into nothingness.

John Keats

8

Happiness is...

living in the moment

Learning to live in the present moment
is part of the path of joy.

Sarah Ban Breathnach

Happiness is like manna; it is to be
gathered in grains, and enjoyed every day.
It will not keep; it cannot be accumulated;
nor have we got to go out of ourselves or into
remote places to gather it, since it has rained
down from heaven, at our very door.

Tyron Edwards

Just to be is a blessing. Just to live is holy.

Abraham Joshua Heschel

9

Happiness is...
working in a garden

Working in the garden... gives me
a profound feeling of inner peace.

Ruth Stout

Gardens and flowers
have a way of
bringing people together,
drawing them
from their homes.

Clare Ansberry

Arranging a bowl of flowers in the morning

can give a sense of quiet in a crowded day –

like writing a poem, or saying a prayer.

Anne Morrow Lindbergh

10

Happiness is...
accepting detours
with a smile

Even with the best of maps and instruments,

we can never fully chart our journeys.

Gail Pool

Remember that happiness is a way of travel –

not a destination.

Roy M. Goodman

When one door of happiness closes,
another opens; but often we look so long
at the closed door that we do not see the
one which has been opened for us.

Helen Keller

Walking is man's best medicine.

Hippocrates

11

Happiness is...
listening

Pleasant words are a honeycomb,
sweet to the soul and healing to the bones.

The Bible

People love to talk but hate to listen.
You can listen like a blank wall or like a
splendid auditorium where every sound
comes back fuller and richer.

Alice Duer Miller

You can make more friends in two months
by becoming more interested in other people
than you can in two years by trying to get
people interested in you.

Dale Carnegie

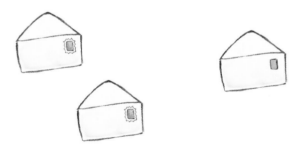

12

Happiness is...
passing on what
you have learned

A teacher affects eternity; he can never tell where his influence stops.

Henry B. Adams

If you would thoroughly know anything, teach it to others.

Tyron Edwards

If you begin the day with love in your heart, peace in your nerves, and truth in your mind, you not only benefit by their presence but also bring them to others, to your family and friends, and to all those whom destiny draws across your path that day.

Anon

13

Happiness is...
remembering your
blessings

Reflect upon your present blessings,
of which every man has plenty;
not on your past misfortunes,
of which all men have some.

Charles Dickens

In the depth of winter,
I finally learned that within me
there lay an invincible summer.

Albert Camus

So live that your memories

will be part of your happiness.

Anon

14

Happiness is...
encouraging each other

He who sows courtesy reaps friendship,

and he who plants kindness gathers love.

St Basil the Great

There are only two ways to live your life:

one is as though nothing is a miracle;

the other is as if everything is.

I believe in the latter.

Albert Einstein

God has two dwellings:

one in heaven,

and the other in a

meek and thankful heart.

Izaak Walton

15

Happiness is...
giving

Blessed are those who can give without remembering, and take without forgetting.

Elizabeth Asquith Bibesco

Spread love everywhere you go... first of all in your own house. Give love to your children, to your wife or husband, to a next-door neighbour... let no one ever come to you without leaving better and happier.

Mother Teresa of Calcutta

Kindness is more important than wisdom, and the recognition of this is the beginning of wisdom.

Theodore Isaac Rubin

16

Happiness is...

prayer

For prayer is nothing else than
being on terms of friendship with God.

St Teresa of Avila

Lord, thou knowest how busy
I must be this day:
if I forget thee, do not forget me.

Jacob Astley

Lord, help me to live this day quietly, easily.

Help me to lean upon thy great strength

trustfully, restfully.

St Francis of Assisi

17

Happiness is...
priceless

Money never made a man happy yet, nor will it. There is nothing in its nature to produce happiness. The more a man has, the more he wants. Instead of its filling a vacuum, it makes one. If it satisfies one want, it doubles and trebles that want another way. That was a true proverb of the wise man, rely upon it: 'Better is little with the fear of the Lord, than great treasure, and trouble therewith.'

Benjamin Franklin

You won't be happy with more until
you're happy with what you've got.

Angel blessing

It's pretty hard to tell what does bring happiness.
Poverty and wealth have both failed.

Frank McKinney Hubbard

18

Happiness is...
home

Having a place to go – is a home.

Having someone to love – is a family.

Having both – is a blessing.

Donna Hedges

The most important work you and I

will ever do will be within the walls

of our own homes.

Harold B. Lee

There is no need to go to India or anywhere else to find peace. You will find that deep place of silence right in your room, your garden or even your bathtub.

Elisabeth Kübler-Ross

A house is made of walls and beams; a home is built with love and dreams.

Anon

19

Happiness is...

painting a picture

Painting is just another way
of keeping a diary.

Pablo Picasso

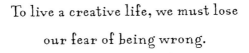

To live a creative life, we must lose
our fear of being wrong.

Joseph Chilton Pearce

There are painters who transform the
sun to a yellow spot, but there are others
who with the help of their art and their
intelligence transform a yellow spot
into the sun.

Pablo Picasso

20

Happiness is...
helping

Any ordinary favour we do for someone
or any compassionate reaching out may
seem to be going nowhere at first, but may
be planting a seed we can't see right now.
Sometimes we need to just do the best
we can and then trust in an unfolding
we can't design or ordain.

Sharon Salzberg

If you cannot lift the load off another's
back, do not walk away. Try to lighten it.

Frank Tyger

21

Happiness is...
realizing the glass
is half full

A pessimist sees the difficulty
in every opportunity; an optimist sees
the opportunity in every difficulty.

Sir Winston Churchill

Trouble is only opportunity in work clothes.

Henry J. Kaiser

It's always helpful to learn from
your mistakes, because then your
mistakes seem worthwhile.

Garry Marshall

I am more and more convinced that our
happiness or unhappiness depends far more
on the way we meet the events of life than
on the nature of those events themselves.

Wilhelm von Humboldt